Letters to Anna

To Love Before Time, To Heal Beyond Hope…

*****

STEVE PACK

Front cover by renowned artist Peter Thomas

ISBN 978-2-9556792-0-3

EAN 9782955679203

CONTENTS

INTRODUCTION

Now, how to introduce a book like this? As this is certainly no ordinary book and difficult to catagorise. I can only describe it as an inspirational autobiography, a special chapter in the lives of two people brought together in unusual circumstances, who share a deep and timeless bond; a bond that helped them navigate and survive a life-storm that could have sunk them.

This book is written from the heart; an act of catharsis and as a means of reaching out to others and offering hope.

While my wife was carrying our first child, she composed a series of letters, written to our unborn baby that contained her thoughts, advise and stories of our lives together and from before we met. I said that I would do the same, but somehow, sadly I didn't.... and then it was too late.

This book is my, belated, 'letter'.

ACKNOWLEDGMENTS

The fire in the jungle raged out of control and as the animals watched in despair a humming bird carried a single drop of water in its beak to quench the flames. Thank you to my close friend Joël who spun me this wonderful anecdote. "We all have a part to play in the world, he said, the more humming birds, the more chance of putting out the fire. Perhaps, he added, this book will be your drop of water, and why stop there, when you have more stories to tell."

Thanks to the great Peter Thomas who kindly offered to pastel our Oak Tree. We're honored to have a such an artist grace the front cover of our book.

To 'you know who,' for your help, genuine interest in the book, the endlessly long chats and for your sense of fun...

When speaking to my father Peter the other day, I let it slip I was writing a few words about him at the start of my book. He laughed and suggested, "Hmmm, beware of this man..." In fact, it's far from the truth! Rarely do we come across someone as charming as him. His sense of humor, un-erring strength in the face of difficulties, his almost unbelievable bravery and his kindness have touched the lives of many! And thanks to my Mum Ros with your boundless love, whose limitless aid to charities and life-long dedication to the Girl Guide movement earned her the 'British Empire Medal' in 2013. She's someone who spent her entire life giving! I couldn't have asked for finer role models... I owe you both so much.

To Daphne and Harry, to grandparents Sydney, Ivy and Eleanor. Ian, Julia, Amanda, Dave and families. All of whom have been so often there for me, with understanding and support.

A huge thank you to my daughter Lilas (pronounced Li-la) for your never ending encouragement, simplicity and directness. You're so precious, so magnificent. Love You!

To Léa, my darling wife, for all we share and for the future yet untold. You have come closer than any other, to knowing the real me. Through your agreement to reveal the intimacy of your letters, you've offered a basis for my story and so opened the possibility to plant seeds in the minds of those willing to listen.

And of course, our dearest Anna. You know my thoughts and how challenging this book has been to write. Thank you for your passage through our lives and everything as a result that we have learned. For all the tears of sadness and all the tears of pure joy! Every second was magical.

1. THE DREAM

Looking down over the canopy of green, trees stretched as far as the eye could see.   Perhaps the thick blanket of forest wrapped all around, covering the entire surface of the earth?

Yes, I had been dreaming in the early hours of morning. But this one hit home with such clarity, that on waking, I sat up with a jolt to reflect on what I'd seen.

As if observed from a bird's eye view I watched and there below, a hooded man, leather bag on back, picked his way steadily and surely in one direction through the dense undergrowth.

Up ahead in the distance, a small circular clearing, within which, a young woman wearing a pale blue dress was alone and waiting.   I noticed the way her long gown fitted her slim form perfectly at the waist.   A silver belt formed a low 'Y' with the tail falling centrally to the ground between her feet.   Try as I might, I couldn't make out their faces... Who were they I pondered and what was the meaning?

I pulled my thoughts back and focus returned again to the man, a medieval traveller, equipped for a long voyage.   He drew closer to what was surely to be his goal.   As I pictured, I felt his intention...   Yes, that was it, his mission to find his love. And when at last he entered the clearing, no words were spoken. They moved slowly, closer and then stopped. Their eyes bathed intensely in one another's presence and time froze... At last the gap between them closed and they hugged, holding on tightly, as if never to let go...

This dream whilst in Canada marked me. Tattooed my soul and kicked me into the realisation that the young woman I had met 7 months earlier was the one. I'd sensed a strange connection from our very first glance, as if I'd known her forever. But now it struck me, this was a message... she was the one in the clearing, deep in the forest of humanity and I the traveller.

2. CHARACTERS INDEED

We had grown up in different countries, different cultures... Although strangely enough, raised with very similar ideas and values.

She was an only child, though never lonely. Animals and Mother Nature presented themselves as thrilling mentors, filling in for the lack of brothers and sisters. Life for this little French girl deep in the Dordogne countryside provided her with no end of discoveries. Every bush held a secret and no rock remained un-turned, never too heavy, never too big or daunting to discourage this girl's curiosity and persistence. Where there was a will, she'd find a way. A true tom boy who's individuality shone as brightly as the sun on a clear day.

Think of the looks on peoples faces when around the age of eight she insisted on taking her pet hen 'Plume' shopping in the big supermarket. As she pushed the trolley, the hen would perch on the front and her mother more than a few paces behind trying to ignore the shrieks of laughter from the other customers. She became well known to the shoppers and some of the old cashiers still remember to this day, the little girl and her chicken.

As she grew, so did her beauty. Oh those green eyes, deep bottomless pools. Could there ever be anyone brave enough to engage in battle holding her gaze? With her chestnut ponytail and a slender but curvaceous figure to die for... Oh, how she shocked her physical training instructors, when in mixed rugby (with the boys), she proved herself to be one of the best players in the school! Sheer determination and unerring belief in herself drove her across the playing field like a runaway train, unstoppable. With only the biggest and bravest of the boys even daring to take her on. Some of whom, quickly found themselves in the casualty ward of the local hospital.

Artistic and musical talents too?... It seemed as if she had no limits.

Hey, but where was her partner in crime? Now twenty-one, of course, still young but she wondered, how long before Mr. Right would walk onto the scene. Could it be that true love existed outside of romance novels? And off of the big screen, out in the real world? Surely yes! She waited for someone, not just to impress her but with whom a true comfort could be found.

She had once drawn up a long list of qualities her future partner was to possess. This list remained hidden, a secret list that only her closest and most trusted friend would ever see. Cheesy perhaps but she knew with confidence that *'timing is everything'*... and he'd come. Even if the years were to roll by before their meeting. Her strength of character would never give up hope... and that hope would set the wheels in motion...

***

On the other side of the English Channel a tall, slim Englishman was already well into adulthood. Behind him lay seven years professional service in the Royal Air Force, in the communications trade and a fair amount of time back office banking in the City of London.

Born into a loving family, things started well for this East Saxon (a nostalgic way of saying Essex boy!), though for his parents it was often financially tough and sometimes they really scraped to get by. Food being carefully rationed and never wasted. He didn't understand at the time but Mum and Dad maintained a moral attitude that love and generosity from the heart, held more value than all the money in the world.

One brother, one sister and grandparents that treated him like a little prince. But somehow, something... something in his blood, gave him a wild side that was impossible to control. Stories would often find their way back home, suggesting that in fact, he was a real black sheep and a rebel.

Thus at the tender age of six he was expelled from his first school for uncontrollable behaviour. It was just that for him, any blame for something he hadn't done was not acceptable and he yearned for apperception. Missile chairs would fly across the classroom towards the teachers signalling his angry frustration. Emotional energy boiled inside, which as a youngster, bubbled just below the surface like a volcano. Also harbouring a vigilante nature, means were always found to bring the loud mouths and bullies to their knees. Not to say that he was out looking for trouble, on the contrary, his heart was kind with good intentions but at this age, a need for justice coursed through his veins.

As he grew, moving through and out of adolescence, his temperament improved and mellowed, becoming more and more aware of how the world worked.

With an excess of energy, lasting passions for weight training and cross-country running were discovered and a solace and comfort was found in books on self-improvement. Books that were to establish solid grounds for later on. A foundation of quiet confidence was under construction, though the drive forever on wards and upwards, searching for love and truth was ever present. So much to experience. So much hunger...

Whenever life seemed to be going so well, suddenly, all went so horribly wrong. Light and darkness swung like the Yin and the Yang, from one side to the other and back again. Balance and harmony beckoned.

But could he find a woman to calm what restlessness remained? One to truly unlock his heart. Buried deep was a hope, that perhaps a character so complex, could be understood.

And using the words of the Deepak Chopra / Demi Moore song 'Desire,' he sent this prayer out into the universe: "Come to me. You have been hiding so long, endlessly drifting in the sea of my love." ... Then, with a deep sigh, he let go, relaxed and patiently waited...

3. MORE THAN A TOUCH OF DESTINY

I'd felt the pull towards France for what seemed like ages. Already, my old friend from the Air Force days had made that jump and was busily starting afresh. And there was I, jealous.

Our regular telephone calls pushed me further and further into a state of craving. Long conversations. Each word like a stroke of the brush, painting skilfully the image of his new life in the French countryside. My desire grew and the temptation became uncontrollably hard to bear. For me, things in the UK seemed to be falling around my ears and my job not nearly paying enough. It was now or never...

Tyres spun, leaving traces on the tarmac that shouted anger at the old ways being left behind and a cloud of burnt rubber lifted and drifted, signalling freedom. With fingers firmly crossed over the wheel, my little grey Austin Healey replica, packed with only my clothes, carried me off in the direction of destiny. Leaving far away, everything I knew. Before long a dull office in London was swapped for endless blue skies, golden sunshine and miles upon miles of glorious green vineyards. And as the French Canicule of

2003 prepared its mighty onslaught, so too my grandest adventures prepared for me their surprises..

I'd promised myself 3 months relaxation before getting stuck into another job and then the plan would be to work in the vineyards. I'd got my contact and the offer of a job already lined up. The stress was off.

My new home, a large white and brown striped caravan sat covered by the barn roof, just down from my friend's house. A view from the bedroom window stretched out over the wide valley below. Oh, those idle mornings in bed, entertained by the sounds of the leaves and bathing in the warm glow that crept through the gaps in the curtains. I loved days such as these. My alarm would be set for 7am and so I'd practice meditation for about 20 minutes and then drift off to sleep again. But the moments between the two, meditation and sleep, often had me confronted by totally new experience, something really strange! And so ensued a long series of premonitory visions. At least 20 of them all in all. How could it be I was capable of seeing glimpses of the future with such exact detail? And then to live them out precisely in the days to come. I saw true colours shining through, clothes, places and sometimes even heard dialogue, all in explicit detail. In the time that shortly followed, they all came to life exactly as I'd seen. Each of these visions realised and experienced in full within one month of having them. That is, *all except one…*

I searched everywhere for the woman in the last vision (who I knew was to be my future wife). I'd so clearly seen her walking outside my window from left to right. Blue coat and platted chestnut hair. I was sat at the kitchen table waiting for her to arrive and uttered three words in English to my companion diagonally opposite me, "Ah, she's here."

But I doubted myself over this particular perception and time marched on, leaving it but a distant memory, unfulfilled. In the following few years other important new events found their way to the loom, that were to weave and shape the rich tapestry of my future. My first serious relationship since leaving England lured me from the Tarn et Garonne to the Dordogne. The harvest of which, saw my daughter Lilas arriving on the scene in the winter of 2005. A precious Christmas gift on a day when tiny icicles clung to branches and frosty leaves shimmered in the sunlight.

Driving to the hospital early that morning, it's safe to say, never have I seen a day more stunning. Mother Nature had scattered diamonds far and wide, transforming the land into glass and glitter; an extraordinary sensation for the first of our senses!

But another 4 summers came went and the relationship with Lilas' mother was showing some serious signs of discomfort for the both of us. Disagreements seemed to be filling up half of our time... She's an incredible woman and a wonderful mother; clear to see why I was *so* attracted. But it was the differences of opinion, that were just too many and too heavy. We both knew that it couldn't continue. Intuition was snapping at my heel and I firmly believed that I wasn't the right one for her. Then blew the wind of change; over coffee break at work of all places.

Courageously I took the bull by the horns, plunging into

the obscure. Only knowing that it had to be done and I prayed that Lilas would one day forgive me. So I made the painful decision to leave, and somehow followed the path I firmly believed was my fate. Rarely had I felt such overwhelming conviction for a certain direction, although it remains one of the most difficult steps of my life.

After my job in the vineyards, I'd then trained as a carpenter. And having mastered just about enough French vocabulary, landed myself a good job with a joinery firm in Bergerac. Each day we'd be building something to kit out garden centres. From display units and suspended ceilings to decking and even cash desks.

At first this was interesting, testing my language abilities and manual skills but after about a year, routine had again started to show its face. For a while all the days seemed pretty much the same and occasionally, I felt a touch of the old 9 to 5 feeling creeping in.

All in all I counted my blessings, though I was still restless. I hadn't yet let go of my need for adventure. (Perhaps I never will). And when two travelling Canadians spun me a plan of how I could taste living in Quebec and give service to humanity at the same time, this opened up a new temptation that became ever present in the back of my mind.

But then it happened... Imagine the scene... Morning coffee break in a man's world. Pictures of naked women on works calendars lined the walls. There we were us men, each with a big mug of very strong black coffee. And there she sat, our new colleague, a rose among the thorns, ignoring the deco, ignoring the taunts, defiantly sipping herbal tea! Our eyes curiously held gaze for a long lingering moment... Léa, the intriguing, alluring French girl had just stepped into my world. Who could have guessed, following my departure from the firm and a 3 month trip to Canada; rings were to be placed on fingers?

Never a truer word in the old saying that truth is stranger than fiction. A big smile creeps across my face when I think how incredible events can be. As Léa and I got to know each other, she mentioned the village in which she'd grown up... The same tiny village I'd been living with Lilas's mum! The two houses were situated within the strong throw of a stone. They were old neighbours!

Then adding yet more icing to the cake, jumping forward to the spring of 2011; there we were Lilas and I, sat in the kitchen of our new house, chatting, and waiting for Léa to return home from work... Have you guessed?

As she passed outside the window, I announced to my daughter, "Ah, she's here"... My vision had been finally realised right down to the finest detail, 8 years on!!! Almost as if re-watching a video, the last premonition played out and when Léa walked in through the door, I just couldn't hold back, floods of emotion filled my eyes. 'Twin Flames,' 'Soul Mates' destined to meet? Or maybe our desires creating our future, creating our fate?

I've said that life can be strange but it's always beautiful if you look at it in the right way. Full of huge letdowns and amazing surprises. How we joked on our wedding day that the 'Livret de Famille' (Family Record Book) we'd been given, actually contained 8 places for our first 8 children. And, that we were to ask for another book if we had more!

"Let's try for 10!" we exclaimed with huge smiles... Oh, the painful irony following that very statement.

Nearly two years had passed since Léa and I first started trying for a baby. She so wanted a family but we tried and tried and nothing happened. I'd sometimes catch a look and noticed she'd been crying, wishing on a star but pleading, why oh why? With our hopes all but depleted, we gave up and did our best to forget. Turning our attentions in other directions, enjoying the hand of cards that we'd been dealt. Anyway, our recently purchased house needed renovating, begging for so much work to be done. The land too needed clearing and tidying. Projects mounted in high numbers. More than we could count. So we kept ourselves busy.

Then, almost as if the stars were sending a reply, a gift arrived. A surprise that stopped us in our tracks: Ooops, no monthly period... And, wow!... the pregnancy test confirmed our deepest desire.

It was November 2011 and my wife came up with an idea. Not to keep a diary but from time to time, write a letter during her pregnancy. Letters she would read out aloud to our unborn child and then be souvenirs for the future. Each day we live stories without words, though we should never underestimate the value of the writing... And so, she wrote: Letters in the name of love. Letters of escapades. Letters to say, 'I will be there.' Letters of guidance... French is such a beautiful language, romantic and poetic. The deeper I immerse myself, progressively the more impressed I become. I sincerely hope my careful translations of her correspondences do justice, retaining at least some of Léa's truly elegant French charm...

4. NOVEMBER BLOSSOM

November Blossom

For several days, I dream of you,
In thinking, my sweetest one, you are conceived.
In the hope to feel your presence,
All my senses listen,
And no noise can trouble my attention.
Thoughts come to convince me you are there,
Cocooned within my greatest care.
Fruit of a love immense.
Harmony from a union eternal.
You swell in me,
Like – A hymn of passion.
The blossoming flower of my life.

(Léa Pack 2011)

STEVE PACK

5. THE LETTERS

Saturday 26th November 2011

My Dear Little Girl,

You are perhaps in fact, a Dear Little Boy? That we cannot yet know but your father and I sense that you could be a girl…. It's just our intuition. Soon we shall see.

I feel very different for about a month now, even though I can notice only very slightly, a subtle change in the shape of my tummy.

You know, it's funny, I who have always enjoyed eating, have now become difficult. I feel all mixed up in the mornings and no longer have the same cravings at breakfast time.

This is just the beginning of my pregnancy and already I can tell you that from time to time I really sense you are there. Sometimes some little pinches that seem to pull me inside. Today my sensations are clearer than ever, changes are taking place. Your father is so excited knowing you are here and we say, "Bonjour" to you every morning. Sometimes your father places a tender kiss on my tummy and imagines that you speak softly to him in reply. What incredibly wonderful sentiments to know you're inside and how marvellous your father is with me. I feel I could not be happier and I can assure you that he is the best of all the men for me. I'm certain that he will be the best of all Dads for you too.

Here, each day, I feel my heart, so bursting with joy, I want to shout! I find myself saying, "Thank you." every day for the life I have been given? We have both desired you so strongly, wishing and wishing and again, wishing one more time. Today our prayers have been answered. Eternal thanks for your coming into our lives, flows through every fibre of my being.

I'm so looking forward to helping you uncover the marvels of Nature. She is Mother of all and she offers enormous love and riches. Just wait and see.

We will soon have our first doctor's visit at the beginning of December. Perhaps we will discover your image! Perhaps we even get to take a little photo of you back with us? Then, finally we can announce to our loved ones, that you are there.

We have learnt that a healthy attachment between parents and their unborn baby will install the childs first feelings of trust. This is only the beginning of our relationship. Each and every day from this moment forward your father and I will take care to nurture this. So when you are born, you will have confidence that your new world is safe and your settling in will be calm. With this firm foundation of security already in place, if you cry we will know for certain it is something other than lack of attention.

Your father and I have started on a new journey with my pregnancy but each step will be shared with you my dear. We are three on this journey and with the help of Prenatal Bonding you are very much included.

Today, the world is seriously acknowledging the importance of bonding with the baby whilst still in the womb. We've taken time to research and read many new studies that prove its life changing benefits. We both know this is the right way forward. We are sure you already feel our communication but I will also keep up with my letters too. I will soon write again my dear. Oh, I'll have to stop now, I feel I could continue our dialogue for hours and hours.

I send you a huge kiss.

Mum

(Léa Pack 2011)

15th December 2011

My Little Darling,

On the 1st of December your father and I went into Bergerac for your very first scan. We were so impatient to see you. I felt the little vibrations of the ultrasound in my tummy then looked quickly to the screen. I looked for you…. and wow, a circle with a little being attached by a cord on the top…. It's You! We can see where your head is and to my great surprise we see your heart which beats. The doctor let us listen and… the first sound of you. It's strong and so fast! Boom-boom, boom-boom, boom-boom. You measure 14.3mm and I'm just 6 weeks pregnant! Your father and I have given you life on the 22nd of October 2011. Well, that's the doctor's estimation, shortly before your father's birthday. And, wait while I calculate…. 447 days after our marriage. I have waited for you since that moment (and if I'm honest even before)…. I often dreamed that I saw you amongst the stars.

At work there are times when I use a forklift truck; it's a little like a tractor but for lifting and loading heavy pallets and wood. You might think this funny for a woman but working in the wood yard shop it's often necessary. Though now you are with me, I'm really careful to avoid all the dips and bumps and drive slowly so as not to disturb you. My 7th and 8th week are happy ones but it's getting so difficult to eat. I don't seem to digest very well. Actually I have the sensation of not digesting at all. My meals rest high in my stomach! Also, I'm not really sure what I fancy anymore. Certain foods really turn me off but until now I've only been sick twice. Your grandmother, my Mum, was very, very ill with me. Sick so often that once, she even stopped eating for a few days! For her it was in the 5th month that all became well. Your great grandmother however was never sick at all…. nothing! What luck? I asked her if she had any cravings during that time and she replied in all seriousness, Raspberry Liqueur, which she normally hated. It made me laugh to think that my grandmother had had the urge for an alcoholic pregnancy! But she knew it was dangerous for her baby and only had a thimbleful once a month! She gave birth to all of her 3 children at home, as was the norm in those days. I would love, if possible to do that for you. So natural. What privilege to be your mother. I will always be there for you. I want to hold you against me. You and me, skin against skin. It's the moment that I'm waiting for the most. You so close and your father looking on proudly. I have complete confidence in him. I know how he will be close to us when you arrive. We will call the midwife to be with us for security but how joyful this shared moment with your father will be. I know the family privacy will be respected even with a midwife there and I can let go of all worries and enjoy the moment completely.

We have finally taken the decision to have a 'home birth' for so many reasons but the icing on the cake has been following Matt Monarch and Angela Stokes of 'The Raw Food World' on the internet. We follow their news and newsletters and they have recently had a highly successful and stress free birth at home with their daughter Oria. Their positive ideas and lifestyle are truly inspirational to say the least. They also organised a 'Conscious Parenting Summit'. Interviews with some of the world's foremost parenting experts. We have picked up so much from this that we find useful in many aspects of our lives. You too will benefit, we'll guide you through, happy, healthy and enriched.

I am very pleased with the doctor we are seeing. He is very reverent of our desire to have a home-birth; I was really worried that he would be against us, but no... I feel very much at ease with him. What good luck! I left his office with a big smile, his secretary gave us things to read, your scans and a tiny baby-grow in organic cotton for you. I was over the moon.

I have a little confession... When your father went to work in Canada for 3 long months, I bought a little all-in-one outfit for you. Of course you were not even conceived... only in my head and my hopes. It was so early in our relationship; I didn't know how to tell your father of the purchase, the desire had been so strong... But when he understood, he was so touched, emotional and happy with my gesture. At the time your father and I exchanged lots of messages, sometimes hinting at marriage but not actually saying it directly. I know that secretly, we both had the same expectation.

All happened very quickly when I took the plane out to be with him for his last week in that exciting country. Re-united again, he told me he'd hired somewhere special for a few days. So off we drove from Montreal to Maple Cottage in the village of St. Adolphe d'Howard. Perched high on a hill, surrounded by maple trees. So, so romantic, I couldn't have dreamt of a more perfect setting. The cottage exuded a warm glow from the moment we stepped inside. And in the little honey coloured wood clad bedroom with red checked curtains, he lost no time in asking for my hand in marriage. What joy! Then followed a wonderful week of hiking, canoeing and sight seeing and for the last night staying in a tree house. An amorous seven day adventure for two people very much in love. You know, he even paid to change his seating place so we could sit together on our return flight back to France...

We were married on the 4th August 2010 in Bergerac. It was a quick wedding that surprised all the family and friends but when the big love of our life arrives, it doesn't wait! Complications with administration meant that the date had been fixed but right up until one week before, we were sure it would not go ahead! So when the paperwork was finally sorted there was not enough time to make the normal invites. Just my parents, grandparents and our witness for the wedding, our close friend, the marvellous 'Zoune.' In England, no one had enough notice to cross the channel for the big day. But all the same, we had the blessings of your father's parents Ros and Peter, who sent their sincere love and best wishes. It wasn't until later that year, we got to meet for the first time and I felt instantly comfortable with the whole family. Who can resist their big hearts and boundless hospitality?

In the month of July before our wedding, your father and I started our search for a house. Our very first viewing together was the good one. Its incredible how, if we have faith, things can fall into place at the right moment. We even got permission from the owner to have our wedding reception in the garden (before it was ours) and finally signed the contract on the 28th October 2010. We were so attracted to this place, even though brambles and nettles and complete property restoration awaited us. A magnificent piece of land, a hectare and a half with a hill of wild grasses that climb up to the vineyards and village. And such good energy. Our home.

Your father had quit his joinery job to give time to Maison Emmanuel in Quebec, Canada on a benevolent basis. It's a therapeutic, sharing community for adolescents and young adults in need of special care. It was an incredibly enriching experience for him. Although on his return, he found himself out of work and try as he might, unable to secure another job. Subsequently we struggled to get a loan for our house. Most of the banks refused us on only my income... except for one. Phew! We had the excellent luck to have been greeted by a lady who decided to do everything within her power to help our loan go through.

And the seller (what a fantastic man) he too was on our side. After our first meeting he decided that it was us... We were to be its new owners! He even reduced the asking price down low enough to be just within our budget! Since I have been living with your father it seems as if good luck is with us like never before. When we have faith, all arrives at the right time and slots into place. Piece by piece we are given another segment and thus construct the beautiful picture of our lives.

Yesterday evening your father announced he was going to create his own business. The Chamber of Commerce had thrown plenty of big obstacles in our way but nevertheless, he was going to do it. That night his one man company was born. Multi-service including, carpentry, painting, decorating and gardening. A new path and already a good direction.

Soon, with time off work and you in my care, it will be my turn to realise my profession of Cabinet Maker and Designer. Then putting into practice my years of training. The break from my current job and move into my new venture will be beautifully timed thanks to you.

Will you follow in my footsteps I wonder? It's so unusual for a woman to work with wood... I already have many new exciting designs in my head and will endeavour to create only pieces of art that have 'never been seen before'. Beauty and originality will be my driving forces. It will be interesting to re-read these letters in years to come to see just how far I have come since I wrote to you. Will I be recognised/acclaimed, will I have won competitions for my work? You can be sure of one thing: when your mother sets her mind on something, her desire and belief will see it accomplished!

Now it's nearly time to sleep, so I first put my pen to rest and then myself.

Sweet dreams

(Léa Pack 2011)

19th December 2011

My Cutest One,

I am writing to you to say that I was a little worried on Sunday. I appear to have lost sensations of you growing, although I see how round my tummy is getting. These last 15 days I have noticed several new changes taking place. Now, I no longer have morning sickness and no more problems with eating. Hooray! I feel much better overall and also much more energetic. My body is getting familiar with you and accepts your being there. I guess that's why, physically, I seem to feel you less than before? On one hand I'm happy to be more comfortable but on the other, I really miss those feelings. I can't wait for a few more months to pass when you will move with force inside me. Enormous anticipation smoulders. The real consolation is that our bonding is getting deeper by the day. An undeniable feeling that I understand you and that you understand me. It's so difficult to describe but so beautiful.

Chatting in bed last night your father and I said how eager we have been to start our little family. Nine months is good notice to prepare for your arrival, so all our thinking and planning will be productive.

You will be a baby of Nature like I was! It is a huge happiness that fills me knowing that your childhood will be in the countryside. To find yourself in a situation of harmony. You will see that when you are still, calm and have love and peace in your heart, you will notice how all of Nature desires to be close to you. Animals and birds don't run but in fact come to be by your side. Many people imagine they are happier in the cities surrounded by lots of things happening, that's fine, we each are individual and have our own ideas. I think in towns and cities people find a certain security. Everything is close at hand, quickly obtainable and perhaps it's all they know? But if we cut ourselves off from technology, and 'Put Aside Our Identity,' then, a connection to the source of life returns.

Your father was raised in a town but now when he sits quietly with our animals, they all come to him and long to be in his company. If only people would take time to be quiet in Nature, then they'd experience their true selves. We entered this life through the Nature of this world and the link is always there, it only takes opening up to it. Here, for us, we find everything we'd hoped for. A magical oneness.... Shoes and socks removed, barefoot on the grass. You'll learn that Earthing or Grounding (the connection with the earth) brings about healing at a cellular level. This together with the practice of meditation is not only good to completely remove stress but is also a innate 'Anti Aging' process!

These understandings of the natural world are a free gift to you; there for the taking. It is the best we can offer you and of course with our love. You have chosen well the time and place to 'check-in' to this world.

A few days ago your father informed me that next year is an interesting one in the Chinese calendar. You will be born in the year of the dragon like me... Surely not another? My father too, what characters! But maybe you will be a gentle dragon?... He also added that whilst in the year of our sign we will have good luck and can even take a few risks, all will turn out well. For you, it will be the physical entry into a new world. And for me will mark the start of my new business....

My love for your father grows stronger and stronger. You know we often say to each other "I love you more today than yesterday" and with your father it's surely true. Our love never stops climbing higher. I think it must be so rare, a love as deep as this. There are no factors that stand in its way. It's sad when nationality, religion and age can strike fear into the hearts of people. All of these things shouldn't be seen as threats or barriers but instead opportunities to learn about ourselves and the world around us! For me, he is my 'Alpha Male'. His desire to be different, to seek self improvement and to grow. To be better today than he was yesterday and to be better tomorrow than he is today! How many of us regularly update to the latest gadgets, the latest software? Forgetting the importance of updating and improving ourselves!

When we tell people about our love, they look at us with eyes as big as an owl. It's funny to see their faces, some jealous but most in admiration. I wish for you also, to experience the one big love in your life when you are older.

So how will you know when it arrives? Trust me... You will know because there will not be a single question in your mind or in your heart... If you feel it in every fibre of your being, then it is right. It will just flow.

With this person you will feel that they fully accept you for who you are today but have your best interests at heart, in order for you to grow and become even better tomorrow. For to stay put and stagnate is not productive; we need to advance and grow in all areas of our lives. Complacency, you terrible enemy! There is always room for improvement and the knowing that our partner is really there to support if ever we need, is a foundation for success and a major ingredient of true love!

(Léa Pack 2011)

11ᵗʰ January 2012

My little one,

Our last rendezvous on the 8ᵗʰ of January was magnificent. We could hardly imagine that in such a short space of time you would have grown and changed so much! You now measure 6.5 cm and already you look fully formed. We saw with deep emotion your little arms, your legs, your feet, your head and we could even count your fingers. You have a well rounded forehead and a tiny upturned nose. So sweet. You are beautiful! What intense pleasure to look at you.

The doctor pressed my tummy in order to make you move and you turned your back on him, how funny. You then twitched your legs and started sucking your thumb! We really savoured these moments and went back with pride written all over our faces. Your father fulfils me in every way but to feel your presence makes me really ecstatic every day. I sense that you speak to me without words. What a precious connection we have. We received our 2011 'Photobox' album yesterday in the post. It took me a long time to carefully choose the best pictures from last year. We'll do this each year from now on. It's really super, an excellent record; we will show it to you later. When we turn the pages we realise the large number of projects we have already completed in only one year. You know, there are at least as many lined up for 2012, I hope that I can still help your father with my big well rounded tummy! I shall be careful with you, don't worry but it's important to assist your father if I can.

Now the goats have finished off eating the brambles, their enclosure can be moved higher up the land to make space for our vegetable garden. And we have of course, your bedroom to prepare before you arrive. Oh yes, and walls to knock down then re-position in the house. Also a dry composting toilet is planned. Many other things too..

One of our chickens called Grisette ('the not so friendly') laid her first egg on the 1ˢᵗ January and has produced one nearly every day since. Your father makes me laugh as he strokes her and calls her darling as she viciously pecks his hand! I admire his love and patience. But we like her, even with her bad character. Surely you hear them from time to time when we are in the garden and an egg is laid. They call out to pronounce their achievement and are quickly joined by Mr. Piou our cockerel who hurries from wherever he is in the field to say "well done" and to sing in unison with them at the joyful event.

What fun when you see them for real? To run in the grass with all of them following. To throw out the grain each morning, scattering the corn on the ground amongst the frenzy of feathers. And you can also squat down and feed them by hand, the way your big sister Lilas does. So many delights and thrills await.

With a smile and a tender kiss,

Your Mum

(Léa Pack 2012)

1st February 2012

My little darling, it's not a day as good as the others today. I hope that you share my joys and pleasures but are not too affected when you sense my pains. I know they are few and far between but when they concern your father they enter my heart and are not easy to chase away. I will help you understand my feelings. Then you shall not be worried but comprehend that there are also things to sort out, solutions to be found.

Life is incredible, marvellous and complex but sometimes difficult. It is for us all an apprenticeship throughout. The lessons that confront us in certain situations are enough to cause fear. When the river is calm, can we tell from a distance that there is a waterfall that waits? And if we knew it was ahead, would we continue on our course? Those who have taken the ride and found themselves in deep water because of a cascade will often be scared of continuing the journey. Those who stay optimistic and always confident in reaching their destiny take to the river with joy and appreciate each step of the voyage courageously. Plain sailing teaches nothing... It's when challenges bare down; we learn the role of captain!

All this your father knows well but fear can be great. Even when we have overall strength of character, it's possible to experience moments of weakness. It's an animal instinct inside us all; it can be hard to shake off. At times you will see it can even outweigh reason and influences our thoughts where it will. Fear can protect us from harm but it can also destroy. We have to choose when to trust it and when to not. I don't think your father yet understands to which point my love for him stretches? If only he knew, the thought of losing me would never enter his mind; he'd remain in total confidence. But from time to time he gets jealous when other men try to gain my interest. In moments such as these, he hits a low, a deep despair; I don't know why? He is yet to realise that when I have chosen a direction, nothing or nobody can change it. He is the one for me and I'll follow through to the end of our lives!

But today we have a solution to find. Because when fear feeds on an idea, it grows. And if we leave the door slightly ajar its hungry appetite will continue to dine. We do this either consciously or unconsciously but it can become dangerous and take control of our thoughts. When fear has got a hold, confidence is tiny. Though there is something you must know, with confidence we are all powerful, we can lift the mountains, but with fear we die. It puts us into prison; we are banned from laughing, stopped from taking pleasure, our good health obstructed and our force removed.

Thus I have decided to take up the battle against fear to help your father who loses faith from time to time. It is the only thing I can do but I have to learn how to fight, as these feelings are his, not mine. How do I attack them? I haven't yet found that reply. Perhaps, it is down to me, perhaps if I make my own confidence so big, so luminous, it will become infectious enough to contaminate your father. Yes!... Then his confidence may to grow on its own. We could say it's a bit like going to the toilet. You can't do it for someone else but you can encourage them! I imagine my example will make you laugh.

I will finish this letter by saying Thank You! As today you have helped me with a troublesome moment. Who knows, if you weren't there I may never have put pen to paper? Though, in talking to you I have found the answer.

A final word of advice for your future my dear: Learn to Conquer Fear and you can Conquer the World!

I love you so, so much,
Mum

(Léa Pack 2012)

2nd February 2012

My tiny one????

Today we have a rendezvous! We are going to see how big you have grown. The last time you measured 6.5cm so it's possible now you have passed the 10 or 12cm mark.

What marvellous moments yesterday.... We settled down to an evening in bed watching a Ray Mears video. My right hand rested on you, communicating my love my attention and plenty of caresses. I felt your subtle movements inside. Then all at once, 'biff!' Your foot? Wow that one really caught me by surprise and I felt you slide down lower to the right side of my abdomen. That was so sweet! I adore the magical moments such as this! There could be no mistaking your force.

It's your fault I have such a huge appetite since about the 3rd month now. I have the urge to nibble every 3/4 of an hour. So I take loads of fruit to work with us. Clementines, kiwis, apples, pears, mixed dried fruit and carrot cake made with the love of your father. He spoils me rotten! I feel like a princess in his care.

Last Tuesday he made us a delicious omelette. Our chickens all laid on the same day so we collected the 3 eggs. Exceptionally, they seem to be spoiling us too. Dark yellow yolks, fresh and healthy and mmmm what a taste.

We have started putting up the new enclosure for the goats. So much work. I am holding the posts while your father hammers them in. That takes certain amount of bravery on my part, hoping that your Dad is always a good shot with each blow. So far so good... but we have more to go! I think we will keep the size of their park roughly the same and where they are now will become our vegetable garden next year. Oh my, how you will love playing with our cheeky goats!

I want to say it's a thrill to write to you my thoughts and experiences. I want you to know all, to feel our love and connection with you. Since the 22nd October, the day of your conception, you have been with us. Birth is not the start of life. Conception is the beginning and physical birth a continuation on another level. You are with us each step of the way. We include you in our conversations and send you our emotions. I believe that very few moments arrive when we are not aware of you and you of us!

Our involvement with you now at this early stage of development will ensure the best beginning for you. Babies that experience this connection grow to be balanced and happy, confident and secure adults. This has been scientifically proven through so much research on the subject. Just imagine if all parents connected with their unborn babies in this way.. Then each new generation of children would have the best start possible! It's such a simple step for each of us to take towards a more harmonious world!

With my love always.

(Léa Pack 2012)

16th February 2012

My Dear,

You are so active. I feel you move in me several times every day. And when father lays his hand on my tummy you respond. Such a big pleasure for us both.

Last week was a good week for you and me, as I could not work due to bad weather. 15cm of snow that quickly turned to ice. We found ourselves completely cut off because of the steep slippery hills around us. Luckily we had enough food to eat and wood to burn for heating. What followed were some wonderful family moments together. We shared many cosy conversations and laughter in front of the fire, entranced by the orange flames. Your great grandmother Jacqueline just happened to be staying with us before the snow arrived. But as timing would have it, at the end of the week she had to be taken for an important pre-hip operation check-up.

Oh, what a risky little adventure then took place. Off we set in my little green Peugeot 106, but not before your father had prepared for the journey. Tow-ropes, shovel, après-ski boots, warm hats, blankets, first aid box, food and a hot drink in a Thermos. Jacqueline was so surprised by your fathers attention to detail. I think he's been watching too many Ray Mears and Bear Grylls videos! "It's good to Be Prepared," your father says, reminiscent of his time as a Scout. But anyway, the voyage went well. 1st gear, 2nd gear, 3rd gear and the joy of exploring a new landscape fluffy white. An escapade that your great grandmother will never forget.

Last weekend your half sister Lilas stayed with us. She's a pretty little flower bursting with energy. So enthusiastic to observe and explore. You will have such fun with her! She is with us every other weekend and during half of the holidays. I will take time to tell you some more about her in a following letter. Maybe you know her already? Perhaps heard her laughing and felt her hands on my tummy saying hello?

We'll soon have my best friend Blandine visiting for a weekend too. So we shall have a very full house indeed. Let me unravel a bit about Blandine. We started our friendship in early childhood, I was 8 and she was 4. We've always been so close, I can tell her anything. She stood by my side when it was tough with my father and beside me when my parents finally separated. She is forever objective and has an ear whenever I need one, despite her younger age.

What hours of mischief we had as kids making dams of stones and clay in the stream that passed by my house. Just so that we could watch the beauty of the waterfalls we had created. They seemed big to us at the time but then we were so small. Little hands and feet in the cold water, we were in paradise.

I remember when we found kittens that had been born in the barn, how we couldn't resist cuddling them. Oh, and chasing my 2 crazy love-able boxer dogs round and round. My chicken called 'Plume' and... where do I stop? So many super memories! Blandine and I have never once argued or been angry with each other. I can't wait for you to meet her. Surely she will be your Godmother when you are christened!

In tenderness,

Mum

(Léa Pack 2012)

18th February 2012

My Little One,

Your father and I are taking advantage of the bad weather (yet more snow) to do some work indoors. We are renovating Lilas' bedroom, this will soon be your room too my dear. What a lot of work; taking out the old ceiling and replacing all the insulation in which we'd found loads of old birds' nests! We have chosen an ecologically friendly insulation and covered it with wood panelling. Mmmm, nice and warm for you. The walls have had some fresh plaster and will soon be painted.

Your sister is asking if she can help with the room. She loves painting and with your fathers' encouragement she learns and gets better each time. She looks hilarious in your Dad's old blue shirt which reaches down to her ankles! Hopefully in a few weeks we will attack the flooring. This is in bad condition; there are even a few holes through which we can see the kitchen below!

You will be pleased that I have drawn the design for a bed for you and your sister. In fact bunk beds. But to start with, you will have a little oak cot which we will make. What good fortune you have, that your parents are talented! When finished, your room will be so adorable.

With each moment that passes, the connection between us deepens. You are growing to accept, and we believe understand the non verbal communication we share. My directed thoughts often have you responding with movements as if in reply. Though I'm careful not to overdo it and respect your need for sleep. That makes me think, perhaps, if we convey 'goodnight' to you before we close our eyes; you will understand when it is night and time for us to rest. So when you *are born a rhythm will already be in place. It's an honour that we seem to be in constant awareness of each other and your Dad says that he can sense you even from a distance. What joy! This is a solace that will grow with you, continuing through childhood and adulthood; a calm reassurance and secure attachment that will guide you on your journey.*

Avec amour

(Léa Pack 2012)

22nd February 2012

My Cutest One,

Springtime will soon arrive, it certainly feels that way. Ever since the snow melted it's been warm and the migratory cranes in their passage over our house have announced that good weather will soon be here. They often circle just overhead gaining height in the warm air and squawking "Hello down there!" before moving on. We saw 4 flights pass yesterday. Huge formations in the shape of arrowheads, thrilling, especially when they're flying north Spring is my favourite time of year. New life everywhere!!!

Lilas is on holiday with us for the whole week. Every day she asks if I have felt you moving inside. The other evening whilst eating a soup dinner, she questioned, "Are there vegetables in this?" I replied "Yes of course." "Ah.... she said, that's good and necessary!" I asked her why her comment and she pointed at you in my tummy. And yes, she's right. She knows fresh vegetables are good for our health and hopes that I feed you lots and lots! I'd like to add that I believe the importance of eating 'seasonal and local' foods are one of the biggest but perhaps understated health benefits known!

Lilas is now 6 and is growing up well, a real pleasure to be with. She's already aware of so much in this world... At times it can't be easy for her but she adapts nicely to the different ways in two families. I sense that she really enjoys her visits to us. It's clear that she feels the warmth in our house. She's a generous and kind girl with a big heart; so often surprising us with gifts. Feathers found in the garden find their way into our hair, to dress us as Native Americans. And pictures appear from behind her back that she has drawn for us. So often with, "I love you Papa," or, "Léa je t'aime," somewhere in the design.

It's clear that she receives the attention of her parents and step-parents on both sides. Sunday should be fun for us all. Off to spend a day by the sea at La Dune du Pyla, Arcachon. You will perhaps sense the salty air for the first time and I'll be certain to convey all that I experience, so you can join in too. It's strange but somehow I think that what I see, you also see? I hope the sun will chase the clouds and we can enjoy climbing the dunes and walking along the beach. We'll take our camera so the photos will show what a beautiful big bump you are in my denim dungarees! Soon a trip to England is planned. It will be lovely for you to hear the voices of your English side of the family. Your father's sister will be there from Australia with her husband and two lively boys. We're looking forward to linking up with everyone, so you'll be overwhelmed by the presence of all your cousins, aunts and uncles and the admiration of your English grandparents.

We have our next doctor's appointment in two weeks. How impatient I am for each and every visit. When I told the doctor last time that I feel you move, he didn't believe me and said that it must be my imagination! But I know for sure! I've been sensitive to you for more than a month now! There is certainly no doubting! Maybe my decision to be connected with you from the beginning has heightened my awareness? For me I felt you move at three months! I don't think it's bizarre for a mother to sense her baby. Oh, there you go again, another kick. Was that to prove the point my dear? You are obviously in good shape, strong and healthy.

This evening your father is working on his plans for a Poele de Masse (Rocket Mass Heater) for our workshop. He's put in so much research already and is now convinced he has arrived with the best design for a home build. This is the most ingenious DIY heating system I have ever come across. It will burn scraps of wood at an incredibly high temperature for about a 3 or 4 hours and then retain heat in the storage mass for up to 48 hours after. So when the workshop is insulated it'll be comfortable for me to continue my cabinet making in the chill of winter to my hearts content.

Two nights ago I dreamt of you. I could see you in all your beauty through my skin. All the details of your tiny form were visible. It was as if you were wrapped up in a vacuum pack. A bit strange I know but superb. I was able to see you, feel you and even cuddle you. It's magical to have you living in my tummy. Nature is incredible!

Mum

(Léa Pack 2012)

Picture by Lilas (2012)

21ˢᵗ March 2012

Hello to you my little GIRL!

So it's affirmative, just as we imagined. The last scan showed us clearly that you are a beautiful little girl. What a relief because we really couldn't come up with any boys names at all! We take a quiet moment with you every day, to give you soothing massages which you simply adore, clearly by your responses! It's either me or your father who gives this attention. The contact your father has with you is just as important as mine. I love the way he connects with you. You already know him well and feel assured when you hear the sound of his voice, the warmth of his touch.

Our holiday to England was great. So you had your first trip in an aeroplane, I bet that seemed strange, with the loud noise and vibration of the engines! At 5 months you are already well travelled, part of the very young 'jet set!'

It was my birthday during that week and everyone chipped in to buy me a professional camera. Lucky me. I feel as if I'm being smiled upon from above. Photography has been an interest of mine from a young age. Now, I'll be able to take some super portraits of you. Also to turn out some high quality macros, I love to expose some of Natures secrets. An evocative beauty which, from our normal perspective often remains hidden.

The windy day at Southend-on-Sea was a real delight. It was a bit overcast but we still had good views of the Pier and out over the estuary. Southend has the longest pleasure pier in the world, 1.3 miles long! Your father tells me that it may be in danger of closure because of the high costs of upkeep. This would be such a disaster for the local tourist trade. They should promote it more, maybe get a donation from a rich person or start a save the pier fund? We will hopefully return again when you are older and treat you to a clickety-clack train ride down to the end of the pier and a blustery promenade to see the lifeboat station.

You'll adore the coast.

Breathing in the salty air with the seagulls screeching overhead and the enticing smell of seafood wafting in from the Cafés along the front. It's easy to understand why your Dad misses the coast so much and all of its sensations. I chatted for a long time to your Auntie Amanda. We sat ourselves on the beach and discussed things from a mum's perspective. We got on so well and I think how good I feel with all the family. If only we could spend more time together.

Back at your grandfather's house that day, Peter asked me to tell him when you kicked, as he was interested to feel you move. There we were sitting on the sofa and I said "she's moving". Wow, the shock on his face when you showed him what a powerful baby you are. It was a wonderful and funny moment that will remain in my memories.

Before we returned to France, we had a special celebration for your grandmother Ros on Mothers Day; a meal at a lovely restaurant in Leigh. Incredible, all of the family was there. All 16 of us stretched around a long table, perfectly presented with candles and decorations. And to our delight, a fancy box of chocolates was offered to all the mothers, even for me too, the expectant mother!

So, my dear... tell me, what do you think of chocolate???

Mmmmmmmmmmm, me too!

(Léa Pack 2012)

31st March 2012

My little darling,

I want to write to you about happiness and I want to tell you that happiness fills me to the point of overflowing! "So Mum, I hear you ask, what is happiness?" Well, I believe it's when you know your life is good and you just can't help smiling. People often use the expression 'to find happiness...' Though I don't think it is 'found' or stumbled upon, I think that it's created! It is us who are responsible for our own situations by what we imagine and put into practice, thus, ultimately creating our own destinies.

How many people think that if only they had their favourite car, lived in their dream house, or were very rich, that this would make them happy? Only to find on receiving exactly what they'd sought, that the 'Happiness Factor' was still, actually missing. So they go searching for another acquisition.... "If I just had that, then I'd be happy...." But stop, wait. It's so much simpler than that. Give someone a big smile that's straight from the heart and your likely to get one in return. What's the visible indicator of happiness? A smile! It all starts right there. Our intention to create happiness by our giving will start abundance flowing in our lives. Simple steps like smiling and performing little acts of kindness each day and you are really on the road to happiness!

Your father and I have noticed that by first giving and then openly receiving, it creates an unbroken universal flow of energy. Giving and receiving are two very important keys and you'll see when we're happy, health, love and wealth are all attracted.

And it seems that the more we give thanks to God or to the Universe, the more we receive in return. It's so strange but true that being grateful for something actually seems to attract yet more of what we are grateful for! We so hope that when you're grown up, you too will practice this loving flow of energy and manifest wonders into your life.

I know that you sense the joy in my soul, with each and every day. But I hope that on hearing these words or one day reading my letters, they will be not just a journal of our thoughts and our lives at the time but also a valuable source of inspiration and guidance!

Your loving Mum

(Léa Pack 2012)

20th April 2012

My Petite,

Seems like a while since I my last letter. My tummy has really swelled and when you're in certain positions we notice bumps of you pushing to find a comfortable place. I can determine when I touch, that I am caressing your head, your feet, your tiny bottom or your hands.

At our check-up comments were made that you are very beautiful baby. The Doctor said that you seem to be one of the healthiest, well formed babies he has ever scanned!!! At the moment though, you have your head in the upwards position. He said that you will soon have to turn around and keep your head down. The doctor informs us that there is a birth preparation class that we can attend each Thursday. I told him that it was kind to offer but "No thanks." He fell about laughing and said that my response was direct, honest and unusual!

After our meeting with the doctor, I sent you a message to tell you that you need to change your orientation and you did so immediately! Such is the connection that we have between us... This is an incredible bond that we have established. But I feel you turning every day. It seems you are not yet ready to settle into your definitive position.

I've also noticed quite often, that when I find myself in the company of someone that I either don't like or do not feel comfortable with, that you remain completely still during these encounters. It's as if you're hiding, trying not to be noticed! I wonder if you have your own intuition or if you're picking up on my sentiments of insecurity. But whatever the reason, I have to say that it impresses me.

I wish that all mothers would join in harmony with their babies the way you and I have done! Our connection, our communication is nothing short of magnificent!

I'm driving over to pick up your big sister this evening who will spend the weekend with us. Your room is still not yet finished but don't fret, it should be soon.

The goats will be moving into their new enclosure before long. So we've had to ask a contractor to dig out a pond on the land. The work has been going on for a few days now and they've dug down much deeper than we imagined. 5 meters! That means rather a lot of earth round the edge that needs to be landscaped into something nice.

We are going to fence through the middle this long pile of earth. Flowers, plants and a dry stone wall will someday decorate our side of the fence. For the moment there is not much water at the bottom of the hole but the level is increasing each day. The ground here is mainly clay so should hold onto the water when it rises. Don't worry as the pond will be inside the animal park and protected from wandering babies. My lively little one, I'm sure you will be full of energy and your Mum and Dad will have to keep a good eye on you. Judging by your movements in me, you will surely know how to run before you can walk!

One of our chickens 'Brunette' has been incubating four of her eggs for about a week now. She's dedicated to her task and doesn't even venture out to eat anymore, so I give her a good handful of grain every morning. Definitely our favourite hen. Tame and gentle and we have to giggle at the funny sounds she makes. Mr. Piou our adorable cockerel has become so protective of his hens. Seems he knows there are chicks on the way and occasionally warns me that he's the Big Boss.

Your sister is being extra careful with him as she knows his claws are sharp. Although the goats also know he's the Boss we don't worry for the two of them. The cheeky rascals often tease him, getting close and then sprinting off up the field out of reach.

Work-wise, your father has enough to keep him busy each day but it's a bit vexing all this spring rain that's falling. Shower after shower, causing havoc with his planning and the outside jobs needing to be put back.

It is now springtime and normally high season for our sales at my work in the wood yard.... But.... zero clients, they must all be staying indoors, frightened of getting wet. The days are so long, they drag with not much to do. So I chat to you when no-ones around.

My replacement has been with us for just over 3 weeks and is picking up his job very quickly and thoroughly.... Little does he know that it's good he's learning fast, as, after your birth, I have no intention of coming back!!!!

Ha ha!!!!

(Léa Pack 2012)

6. AN UNEXPECTED TURN

On Sunday morning the 22nd of April 2012 'Earth Day' a bombshell arrived for us all... Léa went into labour.... exactly 3 months to the day, too early! The 'Due Date' was the _22nd July_ (remember this date for later, it has a striking significance).

The waters broke and emergency services were called. With Lilas in my car we chased the speeding ambulance and rushed to be by my wife's side on arrival. It all took place so quickly. Kneeling on the trolley, still in the elevator, Léa reached down to catch our baby. The doors opened to a flurry of nurses and doctors. The cord cut and our little one whisked away before even having the chance of a proper cuddle.

"It's too early, she's too premature, she has to be airlifted to the specialist unit at Bordeaux," they said. What's her name? Quick, every second counts!" "Anna.... Anna Rose Pack," we replied together.

The incubator prepared, breathing tube inserted, drip connected and a multitude of injections given. Suddenly removed from the comfort of her mother's care and communication, the extreme tension in the air must have been incredibly frightening for our little baby. She'd become so sensitive to what she knew, so secure. Now separated from her mother, could we even begin to understand just how hostile this new environment was to her? The shock must have hit very hard indeed.

Reaching out helplessly, we said a fast goodbye as she was rushed to the waiting helicopter.

With the firm assurance that my wife was comfortable and out of any danger, Lilas and I hurried off to be with Anna... 90 kilometres by road. On the way, a phone call to Blandine who dropped everything to meet us at the other end.

Though when we arrived and tried to enter the word, we were stopped in our tracks. It was parents only. Lilas was not allowed in! Without hesitation Blandine offered to take care of her; as long as it took, until we could get her back to her mother.

Walking onto the ward, a completely sterile world opened before me. Wash and scrub your hands each time upon entry, slip on a clean blue robe to cover your clothes and don't forget a fresh mask to keep the maximum of germs at bay.

Surprised and traumatised, I sat beside the little incubator wired with the gadgets and tubes of the life support system and I prayed... Holding Anna's tiny, tiny hand I felt her warmth of her skin and for a long while focused hard on the beautiful father/daughter contact. Evening turned to night and I kept my vigil. Saying prayer after prayer and telling Anna all about her precious mother and big sister. No word was wasted, she listened, un-moving, to all my stories. Our house in the country, our goats, our cat with three legs, chickens, the turtles in the old pond, everything I could think of. Returning again to how wonderful her Mum was and how I'd do everything within my power to reunite the two as soon as I could...

As I spoke, I felt as if she understood. I pictured these images as clearly as I was able, trying to send them to her, as if we were watching a movie together. All night long we shared; a return to and a reminiscence of our communications before her physical birth.

At 7a.m. I announced to Anna I was leaving but would return soon with her mother. A pause of absence worth the wait I consoled.

Then a caress of her forehead, a gentle stroke of her hand and I set off for Bergerac, where Léa was going through the many check-ups preparing for discharge.

What relief when the 'all clear' was given and we knew that the three of us would soon be together again. Paperwork all signed, we ran like mad things through the corridors. Startled people hurried out of our way to let us pass as we rushed to the car. By midday, we were there.

With surprising confidence, Léa smiled at me and slid her hand into the incubator. "Everything's going to be alright now my little darling one. Mummy's here... You get strong and we will soon take you home." Tension dropped and a feeling of calm wrapped around us and for the first time, we discovered the physical beauty of the baby we'd created. So cute in every way, so tiny, so deliciously formed. Léa and I uncovered her, a bit at a time, being careful not to let her catch cold as our explorations proceeded. What joy this was for us both, our findings were pure revelation.

***

I'd like to deviate for a second and take a moment to talk about physical imperfections, because I'm passionate to make a point here!

We're constantly bombarded by role models for what society and the media considers beautiful. Though most of us fall way short of those images. I was born with webbed toes. The two toes, second and third, are joined together on each foot. Now this was fine... right up until I found myself at school in front of the other kids in the changing rooms. It was then the pain of being different hit me, with everyone laughing and pointing, saying how good I should be at swimming because I had 'ducks feet.' It then became something I was highly conscious of... For such a long time I hid them, for fear of being ridiculed. But now, I've now become so confident, that I can stand before others and let them notice my faults. (And they are many).

I've learnt to accept my differences and realise that they're all part of the make up of who I am. My glorious individualities! I no longer care what people think...

I love to hear stories of people that turned their differences into advantages and with a positive attitude became highly successful in life. What wonderful lessons these serve. To find a confidence in ourselves, who we are, how we've been made, we become a human being that radiates! It's a confidence that attracts admiration from all those around us. We should never forget just how beautiful and important our individualities are.

I invite you to contemplate what deep emotions stirred inside of me, when Léa and I uncovered Anna's tiny feet... Equipped with exactly the same joined toes. There she lay before us, glorious in her personal originality but also gloriously wearing the same trait as her father. And in the wonder of the moment I imagined her saying "Look Dad, I'm just like you."

Long hours of watching over Anna set in; only broken by meals and short sleeps. How we yearned for the time to arrive when we'd all be out of there and starting the normal family life we'd planned. How we imagined walking out, throwing the hospital doors wide open, proudly holding our baby and heading for our cosy farmhouse where we all belonged...

Three days passed.

7. A MIRACLE EARNED?

In every direction medics scurried wearing deep frowns above their masks. This seemed not a place for smiles and if one was passed, only the eyes would tell. I looked around and became aware that everyone was on their own individual mission. Clearly ours was to hold high our banner of courage, a mother's and father's love.

Approaching us whilst flicking through a large file, "Can we arrange a meeting this afternoon at 2 o'clock?" the doctor asked. "We need to get you up to date with events." The appointment was agreed.

Time to go back to the foyer to juggle up a welcome lunch. So good to eat. Breakfast already seemed such a distant memory and although we tried to hide it, deep down we were tired and emotionally drained. We hurried, both eager to be on time. So, well before 2p.m., there we were outside the office door, admiring photos and reading the numerous success stories of the ward. Testimonies of the babies admitted to this special care unit; some babies even more premature than Anna. Radiant pictures of now contented, smiling, healthy children. And so, so many thank you notes to all the staff, for their excellent work. We stood in the corridor uplifted with hope and eager to see all this behind us. "The doctor's running a little late. Do you mind waiting please?" we were asked. OK, no problem, time to digest more of these cheery accounts pinned to the walls.

Finally he arrived with the nurse that was responsible for Anna's care. We got comfortable and the file was opened. Then it came. The sledgehammer fell with an almighty blow...

"There has been a complication. In the process of checking Anna over we have taken a scan and noticed she has a severe brain haemorrhage. Unfortunately, to a very high extent that she has no bodily functions of her own. Our machines and medicine are doing everything for her. The haemorrhaging is taking over a large place in her head and is possibly still growing. There's absolutely nothing we can do to improve the situation. We are so very sorry but if you both agree, it will be in everyone's best interest to stop the support systems as soon as possible."

At this point, I lost my cool and the two medical professionals cowered on their bench under the onslaught of my verbal attack.... "What? .... No! .... What went wrong?!.... It wasn't supposed to be like this........ Give me an explanation NOW!"

They told us they believed her premature birth had possibly been caused by common bacteria that lie dormant in most mothers. In some rare cases it becomes active and attacks the baby causing the mother's body to go into labour, thus expelling the danger to the mother. From there, it's up to the baby to fight the bacteria, sadly a battle that's hardly ever won at this early stage of development.

I didn't know what to believe or who to believe. Though I did know I could run around like a headless chicken but sooner or later the inevitable was going to kick in. Acceptance and a quick decision were sadly necessary.

Time was short now and so very precious. Léa and I rushed back to be by the side of our little one. Both of us from either side, reached into the incubator to touch her not knowing what to say. Silence reigned but our tear-filled eyes spoke volumes.

What can you do in a situation like this? There's nowhere to hide. The doctor had asked for a quick reply, so we negotiated. Yes, we would agree to turning off the support systems the next day, only on the condition that a further scan could give us the proof we needed that this was not an error. We felt so lost and helpless, suddenly so empty. No resemblance at all of the excited little family we had been during the last 6 months. What was happening to all our hopes and dreams?

Calls were made and another scan organised one hour later.

Back with our daughter, we prayed for a miracle to take place, we prayed that she was well and the haemorrhage no longer existed. Or maybe it never had existed, a mistake somehow. So we prayed hard and why not? We were good people, with good intentions, perhaps we'd earned, merited a miracle.

As we gathered around the screen that was to show the image, our hopes were up again. Anxious to say, "Look, you see she's fine; we can take her home soon." They'd brought along our daughter's file to show us the pictures they had taken the night before. We immediately saw the regions that indicated the problem. And yes, the file and the images were clearly marked Anna Rose Pack.

And so, the scan begun. The sensor moving over her head... Revealing... oh no, even more shadowy patches than before. The haemorrhaging had spread, overpowering all of our dreams and taking control of her fate.

A huge dark cloud of despair swept through the ward.

8. THE OLD OAK

The next day, awareness of every second was so important. I remember so clearly sitting beside her. It had become a little habit for me to place my finger in the palm of her tiny hand. I communicated with her, sometimes verbally, sometimes spirit to spirit like we had done when she was still in the womb.

At one point I spoke to her out loud, "You know, I really, really love you Anna." and with a surprise shock that left me reeling... she gripped my finger tightly as if in reply!!!!

Up until then our fingers had rested in her hand just touching her palm, never a single movement on her part, not even a reflex. This was a firm squeeze! This was strange but beautiful. Don't ask me for an explanation, I don't have one but there it was, as true as can be. In all the time since her transference to Bordeaux, she hadn't moved and here she was gripping my finger, telling me that she loved me too!

I concentrated hard and with all my strength, pulled my focus into the here and now... Anna, my darling daughter,

I said, for whatever reason destiny has been cast. The dreams we had of our family, of experiencing your childhood, this evening will be taken away... Our earthly time together is coming to a close... So, somehow, I'd like to try and share a special moment together with you right now. A moment that will live on forever...

Let's imagine you are eight years old..." I closed my eyes and imagined hard. Suddenly, there she was standing before me, beautiful, cheeky and giggling. And wow, was she beautiful?

With my eyes still closed I said, "OK, Anna, you know the big old oak tree where I carved the heart for your mother? On the lowest of its mighty branches are two ropes for swinging. We'll race to the tree and the first one to climb to the top of a rope and touch the branch is the winner. The loser has to bake a chocolate cake for the winner. Are you ready, steady, go..."

I saw us racing with the wind in our hair.... The grass before us a rich green carpet, the trees silhouetted in clear blue. And standing out amongst them I saw the old oak, waiting to greet our folly. Chasing up the garden we went. Like a good Dad, deliberately letting her pass in front. Up the ropes, hand over hand the two of us climbed. Stretching out above her, she reached to touch the branch, just before me. "Ha ha, she squealed, you're making the cake Dad!"

This sharing, this play, felt so very, very real. The two actors took to their roles and portrayed their finest performance. Both determined to make this, a scene, never to be erased...

9. TIMELESS

Timeless

When quiet and calm surround my being,
And wandering thoughts run free.
Imagination's all it takes
And there she stands with me.

Excitedly she beckons,
With laughter in her eyes.
"The oak tree's there and waiting Dad,
Let's race again!" she cries.

(Steve Pack 2012)

STEVE PACK

10. COCOONED

So Léa and I made our way back to the foyer to ready ourselves for the fateful evening ahead. Words of reassurance were passed back and forth between us, attempts at bravery. But it was the many hugs that helped the most. For we knew there was no escaping what awaited.

Then, the walk back to the ward, step, by difficult step. And a gentle rain fell.

A private room had been prepared. Where beyond those doors, the outside world ceased to exist. As if trapped inside a bubble where nothing else mattered. Dimly lit, strangely, almost as if by flickering candles. Two comfortable armchairs, little Anna in her incubator and the uncaring clock on the wall, counting down.

8 o'clock arrived. Our wish to be able to hold her in our arms for the first and last time had been granted. Skin against skin, as natural as possible. Physically united. A mother's right, a father's right, just *to be* with our child. Shirts removed, cuddling our naked baby. Serene... "It'll

be quick, they had told us. Without connection to all the support systems, she'll pass on rapidly..." But rapid? ... This was not to be the case.

Someone up there granted us yet another moment of pure wonder and beauty. This was grace, this was a true blessing. Oh how we relished every precious second. So warm and cosy, snuggling into our chests. Again that feeling for Léa returned, as in her poem, her baby 'cocooned within her greatest care'...

"Anna, I said, our time together has been so fulfilling but so short. Thank you for all you have shown us... I hope sincerely that our souls will meet again!" And then came a second sharp, confirming, tight grip of my finger which gave me her reply!!!!

For two gloriously long hours, we all cuddled together. Our little desperate family holding on with our big smiles and our big tears, until our tiny angel flew.

11. PICKING UP THE PEN

My Dearest Little Anna,

Tonight I pick up my pen to write to you again, after a break of several months. I think of you every day since you have gone and I miss you terribly. Although I don't want to hold you back from your journey. So I try to retain some of the tears and the sorrow in my heart.

My pregnancy with you went really well apart from having quite acute tummy pains on two occasions. Although during those particular pains I was never worried for you. These were familiar and I remembered having the same sensations during my childhood.

We connected soon after your conception and I felt you moving in me very, very early on. A perfect harmony was experienced together, all the way through to your birth. Mere words are not enough to describe this connection between us that was equally felt with your father.

On the Sunday 22nd April my first contractions started whilst I was still sleeping, at about 8:30a.m. I then had to change positions every five or six minutes due to the discomfort. On waking I was a little worried about the strong pains in my lower back. Soon after, I lost some amniotic fluid and rushed into the bathroom where I lost even more. Not panicking, I took time to clean the floor. Then went back to tell your father. Contractions came every five minutes and quickly then every three.

I felt best being in the all fours position on the bed. The strong urge to go back to sleep was nearly overpowering but the contractions were stronger. Your father and I discussed if we should call for help because you were only six months formed. In the back of our minds our desire for a home-birth was still present and perhaps, anyway, there was not enough time before you arrived. But safety took precedence and the joint decision to call the ambulance was taken. The call was made at 9a.m. and they arrived at 10:30. From this time on I stayed upright but on my knees, right up until you were born.

Your birth was imminent throughout the journey but we remained perfectly connected and I think you held on, knowing this was not yet the best moment. As soon as we arrived at the ward, still on the trolley, I felt you descend I realised that this was the chosen time for your birth, although much too soon. I thought OK, we have to take life as it comes. It's God who decides when, or perhaps it's you my little Anna who has chosen, so I will not fear.

Your father and Lilas had followed the speeding ambulance the whole time. I could see them from the back windows and felt reassured. In the hospital lift I said, "She's coming, I feel her." I don't think anyone believed me and as they tried to transfer me onto a bed you arrived. You were born in the breach position. Your bottom first, your wriggling right leg, then the other, your tummy and your arms.

But your head stayed until I had pushed lightly just twice more... and you were there! I was wearing a long skirt and bathrobe so our intimate moment was hidden from the world. Nobody saw.

I held you forward to have a good look at my little girl and your father had just enough chance to caress your head. The midwife wanted to take you immediately but I held you to my breast for just a few seconds before accepting their care. You weighed 1.2kg, so perfectly formed, such a beautiful baby.

Darling, you were so magnificent for me. Birth is an act filled with love and happiness. I lived this moment with you without fear, completely and solely in love.

Everything was wonderful.

(Léa Pack 2012)

13ᵗʰ June 2013

Dear Anna,

Today, it's just over one year and one month since you were born and I return my pen to paper again. Here to share my thoughts with you. One year, it's the time it has taken for me to be sincere with myself when I say, "Your absence doesn't cause me pain and I love you more than ever my dear." I feel happiness whenever I think of you and the bubble of sadness that lay heavy in my chest has lifted.

Ever since my childhood, I've been convinced that all of us placed here on earth, have the goal (whether we know it or not) of growing and raising our vibration. As a teenager I thought it was best adopt this frame of mind as early as possible. Becoming aware that my feelings were in no way predestined or evoked, but mine to choose. I began to analyse myself in moments of fear, anger or sadness, and understood quickly that external factors were not responsible for my state, but that it was I who decided the feelings that I wanted to create. What a joy to know that in reality no one and nothing can harm our happiness except ourselves. Understanding this, I thought: life can be such a prankster, everything seems so complex but NO... In fact it's so easy.

During the years that followed this realization, I practiced each day to control my emotions until peace in my heart become a habit. During this period, I was on permanent self monitoring. I regained control whenever I had a bad feeling and tried to calm my thoughts if ever they became negative. Soon the exercise became natural and spontaneous, it was no longer difficult. The emotions of others in opposition affected me less and less because I knew I was not the actual cause. Far from being indifferent, this new way of being enabled me to find the right solutions and interact more easily. I had helped myself, and now I could go on to help others.

When doctors told us that you were condemned, your father squeezed my hand with all his strength. I felt his pain, his anger, his confusion. We were shocked, terribly disappointed to lose you, my first and only child. A thousand questions raced through my mind in seconds: Why us? What did we do wrong? I hadn't smoked or drunk whilst pregnant. This is not fair! Was it my fault that you were born too early?

Was it all the injections by the medics you were given or the stress of you being so suddenly removed from me that caused your haemorrhage? Had I been right to ask Steve to drive us to the hospital or was it best to have let nature take its course at home? Would my husband blame me for that? I was for a while feeling guilty and I noticed the anger on Steve's face as he sought a culprit to blame for our situation. Two different attitudes; me blaming myself and Steve blaming others, these were our first ideas. But then quickly, I brought my focus back to you Anna and I thought we did not have time to waste on these absurd notions. What mattered right there and then was the time we had left with you.

We felt terribly helpless, but knew we had to stay confident in the face of fate. You needed our love and our smiles more than you needed our fears and our tears. I wanted to pass this test, for you but also for Steve who needed me as much as I him. We encouraged and coached each other through this time to be at peace in that difficult situation.

Thus, when faced with your departure we were fully able to enjoy the final moments with you. To smile and send you our love, our confidence and share our happiness. I have the feeling that nothing has been due to chance, and that you are completely blissful where you are now. The other night I was reading the awesome book 'Initiation by Elisabeth Haich' and I read this: 'God loves my child even more than me.' And as I write, these words are ringing harmoniously in my ears.

Dear Anna, your journey with us was so short but it does not remain less rich. We are honored to have known you. And through you, life seems even more beautiful than before. We have attained a higher level of peace and understanding in our lives and the love between your father and I, is deeper still. Your time with us darling Anna was beauty in its entire splendor.

Thank You

(Léa Pack 2013)

12. CHOICES

The weeks just following Anna's departure were really tough; I don't know how we got through them. Could we ever recover, would the clouds ever pass? As for me, I descended into the depths, somehow forgetting the highs I'd experienced throughout the pregnancy.

I remember that the anger and sadness had built up to such a level that I wanted to smash everything in sight. I spent hours wallowing, searching for someone to blame. Somehow, Léa managed to pick me up each time I fell... There she was, my beautiful wife, holding, supporting. But the pain ran deep and the thoughts I had were really dark. I feel ashamed when I look back at the monsters, that for a while took over and dwelled in shadowy caves, where once there had been so much light.

At times I nearly completely lost my sanity. I found myself swimming in circles, in a bottomless pool of pity and depression into which I'd plunged... Léa's positive attitude had been installed early in her adolescence. A golden self-discovery that up-lifted and carried her through the difficult times. It wasn't until she wrote the last letter to Anna a year later that it clicked and I understood why, during the first few weeks, she'd coped so much better than me.

Round and round I swam, feeling that soon, I would surely drown. Until, out of the blue, a thought came to me, almost as if spoken by a tiny voice... (Anna???) "There are really only two ways of looking at life's experiences, you can choose to look at them negatively or positively. The choice is yours. Though if you look closely enough, you *will* find the good!"

Remembering my old character, how I used to be... loosing our daughter could've been seen to be the ultimate injustice! The anticipation of a joyful family with the love of my life had been my heartfelt wish. Then, to be so suddenly torn from us; dramatically snatched away.

These words of wisdom about choosing either the negative or the positive in each situation played over and over in my head. They just wouldn't let me go. So I looked closely... I thought carefully on all we'd experienced... It was then I started to find and to see some good. First in one direction and then another! And yes, the more I looked the more I noticed and realised what we'd mastered and how much we'd been given.

More than anything else, we would have wished for things to have turned out differently, though they didn't and nothing could change that. What was the use of negative, destructive sad thoughts and what damage would they have caused? Damage to both ourselves and to others.

With a strong will and with practice, I was acquiring a new competence. Once more the world lit up, became even brighter, even more wonderful than before!

It's not time who's the healer. Though it would be foolish to say it doesn't help... But rather a certain attitude needed. An attitude that's able to transform, to turn things around. A knowing that we have, in fact become richer in successfully overcoming the obstacles placed before us.

When challenges bear down they become opportunities for us to grow. And it is here we can come to understand, it's not the events that control our lives, it's our decisions.

So often we seem sure we know our direction. We know exactly what we think we need. We want, we want, we desire, we want!!! But life is secretly perfect and when we have faith... then, we can go with the flow. On looking back we'll notice all of the crazy messed up times were in fact, just the path that led us to today. All the difficulties were there to help us grow. And here we are; experiences under our belts, wiser and more fulfilled than ever before.

If we take a moment to place our lives under the scrutiny of a microscope, we'll notice how we're presented with and guided through situations necessary to evolve. Hurdles, problems, temptations.

Do any of us need to be a soldier who falls by the wayside, too wounded to continue. Hope gone, despair the new master, fear the victor. Those who're able to remain positive, march on, faces radiant, grinning from ear to ear! It seems that in every moment we are tested. I don't need to go into detail here, as each person will have their own tests. But trust me on this; we're all capable of passing with flying colours. *If we wish*, help, answers and guidance will come; words of encouragement will be found. Be open and what we need to carry on will arrive.

I've recently been thinking again about the scene I'd created with Anna in the hospital. The one of her and I running to the Old Oak. This was very important for me at the time. Seeming to be a two-fold creation, allowing me to feel something with her, that in reality we'd never be able to live. But also, I'd thought this scene could be replayed if ever I experienced future moments of weakness or missing. The idea was to just close my eyes and she'd be there again… Although I realised later, that having created such a fall back; in fact I never needed to use it.

Thus it served as a 'one of.' A wonderful play which didn't have to be re-enacted, just there as a powerful, beautiful memory of the moment. But as a therapy it would have been an unhealthy one. You have to move on. Life has to keep advancing and not stagnating.

Yes, the moments spent with our little one were extremely brief… but did we miss out? Are we left empty?…. 'Au contraire!!' We remain filled by the beauty of the 6 months and 5 days Anna spent with us. Valuable beyond all imagination. From the very beginning of pregnancy, we communicated daily. We laughed, chatted to her, played her music, sang her songs, shared the sounds and experiences of nature and of course wrote her letters. And she in return responded and gave to us more than simple words can explain.

Finding treasures along the way, we listened, grasped and

put into practice our new understandings. And with the application of Prenatal Bonding we'd reached out and really connected with our daughter, really knew her, even though she was still in the womb! 'To love before time...' It's something every parent can do. This intense connection we tasted opened up another world... One we never foresaw; never knew existed. A new energy, a higher vibration. Yes, the world took on new meaning, never to return to the old. A complete lifetime, lived to the full in half a year! So if you know anyone who's about to become a Mum or a Dad, go ahead, recommend Prenatal Bonding... Research the new discoveries that are being made every day in this field, we can assure you they are nothing short of mind blowing.

For many reasons our story is unusual, unique. Many couples can take for granted an easy conception, a full term pregnancy and a healthy birth. Though it's worth being aware, that life can at any time, take a sharp, new, unexpected turn. We're all transient, we're all just passing through, some much quicker than others.

If only we can become conscious that every second counts and try making each and every second a good one. Filling our time with Love, Kindness, Generosity, Understanding and Laughter. Filling every second with Joy! What a great feeling exudes when we get to the point of knowing we've done our best. And where we've walked, where we've passed, we've left a good mark on the world; constructing magnificent memories along the way. If I sat down to write about my failures and about my faults, surely it would be in excess of a thousand pages. I've done so many things I regret. Wow, have I messed up in the past. I bow my head in admission; I'm so very far from being perfect.

Though here I am today, consciously aware and consciously making an effort to improve, with a will to help others and a will to make changes.

There are times now when I'm able to look in the mirror with a certain poise and say: "I might not be proud of who I was yesterday but I am happy with who I've *become* today."

I realise I've changed and what was pain has now become action. By shifting the focus, I've acquired the ability to turn my attentions outside of myself. Now mastering *The Law Of Giving* takes precedence and becomes the new objective.

We've had some bruises, gained some scars but earned some laughter lines too… In so many ways Anna lives on. She's always there as the glint in our eyes. She's there as a force that drives us on. And once again, as I tap upon the keyboard in the wee small hours of the morning, she's there in the corner of my big crooked smile.

Exposing our intimacy and going public with such an autobiography was at first a difficult decision but then we considered that we all know someone who's experienced loss and could be suffering in silence. Maybe, just maybe this little book would offer a new perspective and encouragement to face the future? I'm glad we gained the confidence needed to reach outside of our cosmos of security, to touch some hearts and offer some hope.

It's easy to see our little girls' passage has accomplished many wonders… a passage filled to the brim with valuable lessons. And if Anna's looking on right now, I can imagine her grinning, knowing how she taught us to love life even more. So awesome the fact that her visit was only 6 months and 5 days but one so influential, 'Letters to Anna' just had to be written.

***

I grew up by the coast. Childhood memories and anecdotes run wild in my mind... But those can wait, I'll save them for another day.

Observations however, merit the place for one last mention and a dedication to Anna that rises inside of me and escapes its bounds; just before we turn the page.

'Not as a splash, with trailing ripples, ever decreasing. Fading... She came like the power of the sea! With every wave, a new beach formed. And like the sea, once experienced... Never forgotten.'

***

We trust you won't take Letters to Anna only at face value. It's messages run far, far deeper than that. So many experiences, so much learned, so many keys to happiness discovered. What an incredibly inspirational journey we've travelled thus far. And as the mist clears... *'We see that the power of 'choice' lies within us all and challenges are always opportunities for us to grow.*

Over four years passed since her departure and actively we tried for another baby, longing for that family of our dreams... But again we waited and waited... Was this to have been our only child together? If so, we'd brave the reality, holding our heads high with confidence, knowing that other wonders awaited. Or could it be perhaps one day we could say, "*Wow!* The pregnancy test is positive!"

Way back in 2010, on the day that Léa and I first viewed our house, I remember so clearly, we were sat outside in the sun chatting to the owners. And out of the corner of my eye, I thought I caught a glimpse of our future daughter. Crawling on all fours, wearing white smock and trousers and strikingly blonde hair. How strange I mused, as my wife and I are both very dark. It was so profound, I couldn't resist telling everyone present and we all laughed at how ridiculous it seemed. But was so ridiculous, or was it yet another of my premonitions?

After all of our trying for another child, out of desperation we finally got in touch with a fertility specialist who agreed to take us on her list. A whole year of checks and tests then followed until Léa and I got to the point of exclaiming, "This is too much pressure, too much stress. Enough!... Let's *stop* worrying and relax, what ever will be, will be." Have you ever been in a situation of genuinely giving up and letting go? Completely surrendering to the universal scheme of things (but with faith)? Well just before the process of artificial insemination was about to begin, that was exactly what we did and took a fabulous holiday back to England. Fun and relaxation indeed.

Family, friends and the delights of exploring the rugged but beautiful Cornish coast. A part of England in which, my Grandparents as youngsters had shared so many romantic holidays…

As we're drawing to the close, I feel compelled to say that throughout the writing of this book, *somehow* I knew it would end happily. Even in those darkest of moments, something deep inside of me still held on. Like a light from within, it was always there…

***

'Now look towards the skyline, face garnished with a smile. As the deep blue of the night subsides, subtly transforming with the first rays of sunlight, a new day begins. What joys and surprises could be waiting just over the horizon? Adventures, eager to share their secrets with those who learn how to chart the course and all those who truly believe.'

17th November 2017

My Dearest Baby Daughter 'Jade'

Wow, what a surprise! Welcome to our world! After all that we've been through, you are here. Little Miss Made in England, Little Blondie Girl!

Little Miss 'Jade Pack,' born on the 22nd July 2017. How delightfully curious; I wonder why you chose 'that' particular day? The very same day your sister Anna was due to be born !!! The universe can indeed bless us all with miracles.

Your mother has always said, anything is possible, if you really believe in your dreams.......

(Steve Pack 2017)

Printed in Great Britain
by Amazon

44435452R00050